Managing Organisational Change

a management workbook

Paul Tarplett

and

Laurie McMahon

Office for Public Management

inside managing for social result

Managing Organisational Change is the second title in a series of workbooks for managers, *Inside Managing for Social Result*. Other titles include: *Managing Strategy* (1998) and *Managing and Developing Others* (forthcoming).

Series editor: Paul Tarplett

Editing & design: Leila Carlyle
Cover image: PhotoDisc
Printed by WCS Digital

OPM

252B Gray's Inn Road
London WC1X 8JT
tel: 020 7239 7800
fax: 020 7837 5800
email: office@opm.co.uk

ISBN: 1 898531 48 X

Contents

List of Exercises

Acknowledgements

We are grateful to other members of the Office for Public Management, particularly Ian Gee and David Albury, whose work has contributed greatly to the *Inside Managing for Social Result* series.

Foreword

The roots of this workbook are in Dick Beckhard's models for managing the change process and his research and applications on managing organisations in transition. Dick, one of the founders of organisational development, has been a friend and advisor to the Office for Public Management since its establishment.

The Office has been building upon and applying Dick's concepts of change management in learning programmes and consultations for a number of years. In particular, our seminal work in designing large scale, open simulations has been employed in managing complex change across the public services and increasingly in the private sector.

This workbook has been created with Dick's help to provide tools and guidelines for the ever increasing demands from organisational leaders for assistance in managing complex change. We gratefully acknowledge Dick's help and support.

Greg Parston

Chief Executive,
Office for Public Management

Introduction

This is a workbook for managers and others with managerial responsibilities in public service organisations who wish to develop their understanding and skills in the management of change. It emphasises the social outcomes or results that public management aims to produce and how these can be achieved.

It will be particularly useful to managers who are required to manage change projects from start up to conclusion, providing them with a step-by-step guide on how to do this. However this workbook will also be of use to those wanting a general understanding of change projects and the theories which underpin good practice. The workbook is intended to be used as a self-taught module or to support a facilitated learning programme about organisational change.

Objectives

The objectives of this workbook are:

- **to explore the nature of organisational change**
- **to provide a framework within which desired changes can be identified, planned and managed**
- **to introduce a range of tools and techniques for managing organisational change**
- **to explore how people respond to change and provide guidance on how they can be helped to deal with it**
- **to examine resistance to change and how to manage it**
- **to provide an opportunity for managers to reflect on their development needs in relation to managing organisational change.**

Using this workbook

This book is intended to be used as a practical tool to help you extend your knowledge and understanding of change management. It is structured to provide you with a range of ideas and practical approaches to organisational change. These are reinforced through a series of exercises. Although you can do the exercises on your own, they will be more valuable if used as part of a group training or development programme and/or discussed with a colleague, mentor or training manager. This 'supporting cast' will be particularly important for individuals working alone. You will get a lot more from the exercises and the book if they are used as the basis for discussion with other people.

Most of the exercises include some space to write in your responses. ***But don't feel limited by the spaces allowed***: they are not meant to be a guide to how much anyone is 'supposed' to write. In any case, if you are using the exercises with a group, you will want to use whiteboards or flip charts to gather people's responses.

The book is designed so that you can work through it systematically, applying it to a particular change problem, or if you wish you can pick particular topics of interest and work on them, in the order that suits you.

For example, towards the end of the workbook there is a section on how people respond to change. Some people find this a good place to start, thinking about the impact that change has had on themselves and their colleagues before coming back to look at how to plan and bring about organisational change.

The content

The material that might be covered in a workbook on organisational change is potentially enormous and we have had to be selective. We have chosen to focus on the following areas:

- **pressures for organisational change** – the external forces and drivers of change and the judgements made within the organisation about how to respond to these;
- **planning for change** – assessing the present situation, clarifying change goals and deciding how the transition will be managed;
- **implementing changes** within the organisation;
- **understanding the impact of change** on the various individuals and groups who have a stake in your organisation.

The book is particularly concerned with managing the human aspects of change, because this is where most change projects fail. It is not a work-book on the specifics of project management, although the general approach would provide a useful frame-work for programme management.

This workbook as part of a series

This is the second workbook in our series *Inside Managing for Social Result*, the first of which is *Managing Strategy*. Change requires us to think about the future – which is also the purpose of strategy – and so it would not be surprising to find a degree of overlap between these two workbooks. To minimise this overlap, references to *Managing Strategy* are made where appropriate. Each workbook, however, is entirely complete in itself.

The book's structure

The workbook is divided into eleven chapters. This introductory chapter begins by asking you to think about what you want to achieve. The next chapter – The Purpose of Change – will help you to think about the different ways in which we can view change – and organisations – and how this affects the way we approach change. It also explores why change is an issue to which we need to respond.

This is followed by an overview of the change process, including the prerequisites for change. This provides a framework for the remainder of the workbook which covers:

- **analysing present problems** – four techniques for examining the present;
- **'visioning' the desired future** – four approaches to deciding what you want for your organisation;
- **creating a strategy for change** – by working at the individual, group, organisation-wide and 'whole system' levels. We outline some techniques that will help to prepare people for change, overcome any resistance they may have, and build the commitment and capacity that people need if your proposed changes are to succeed.
- **reviewing and learning from change**.

In the final two chapters we look at how to manage people's individual reactions during a time of transition, and finally – and very briefly – at review and action planning.

But before you begin ...

Setting your own objectives

The first exercise, overleaf, is intended to help you think through your own objectives. Before you think seriously about changing aspects of your organisation, it is always worthwhile considering what your starting point is and what you are hoping to get out of this workbook. Like all the exercises here, this can be done individually or with a group of others who share your interest in learning about change.

Exercise 1

Personal objectives

To help you get started, spend five minutes identifying what you want to get out of this workbook.

As with any good change project it is important to have a clear set of both organisational and personal objectives before you start and also to review these regularly as you progress, recognising that they may change as a result of your experiences and learning.

One way of starting this process would be to read the workbook's objectives (on page 1) highlighting those that are particularly important to you and adding any other, perhaps more personal, ones in the space below. These objectives could relate to a specific change management issue you are currently involved with, or may be more generally about developing your capacity to lead and manage change.

What I hope to get out of working through this book

....

....

....

....

....

....

....

....

....

....

....

....

....

....

....

....

....

....

....

....

For other prompts to your thinking you might consider and make notes about the following.

- **the role you have**
- **the contribution you currently make to your organisation's strategy**
- **the contribution you would like to make**
- **any experience you have of creating or implementing strategy at an organisational or departmental level**
- **any particular problems which you or your organisation needs to tackle and which you feel should be dealt with strategically.**

....

....

....

....

....

....

....

....

....

If you are working with a partner or a group, take a few minutes to discuss with them what you have written, and to listen to their views.

The Purpose of Change

Talking about objectives ... Before exploring the detail of how organisational change can be brought about, it is really worth spending a little time being clear about what it is designed to achieve. It may be stating the obvious to note that change for change's sake is not likely to be your objective.

Like other organisational objectives, those for change may be intended to work at different levels. If you regard the organisation as a system, such as shown in the diagram, it is possible to set objectives for change at the following levels:

- **changing inputs** – for example, changing the types of people who are recruited into the organisation;
- **changing the processes** by which work is done – e.g. introducing new management structures;
- **changing the outputs** of goods or services produced – e.g. introducing a new type of service such as delivering IT education to adults in pubs;
- **changing the outcomes** achieved – e.g. reduced deaths from lung cancer, improvements in educational attainment, or increased user satisfaction.

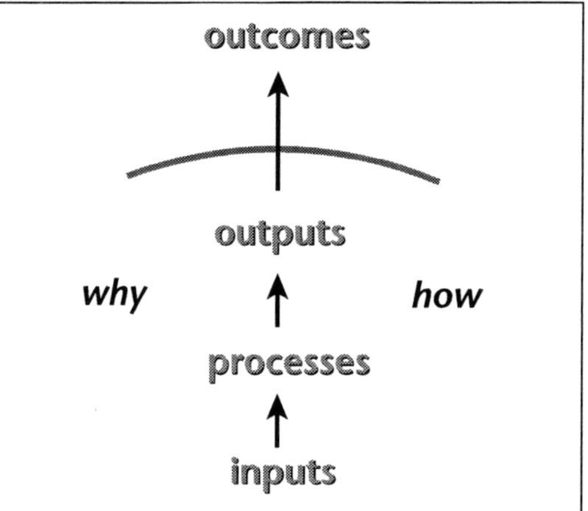

the 'systems' view of organisations

As you set out to change some aspects of your organisation, it is important to remember the fundamental point that your organisation exists to achieve a purpose in the world. It produces outputs (goods or services) that are intended to achieve specific outcomes (whether these are profits, social result, public acclaim, political approval, etc.). In any planned change effort, therefore, it is worth thinking carefully about what effect the change will have on these outputs and outcomes. This will also help you to remember that all the other things you may change – such as structures, communication and decision making systems – are simply a means to that end.

We encourage you to write your change objectives using the SMART criteria. They should be:

Specific, **M**easurable, **A**chievable or Agreed, **R**elevant and **T**ime-limited.

Exercise 2

Objectives for change

Think about a change project that is important to you and ask yourself what it is designed to achieve and how this will affect the outputs to users (customers) and the outcomes your organisation wants to achieve. How will success be measured? Summarise these below, as far as possible using the SMART criteria headings. The example on the left may help.

** we suggest you choose an aspect of your organisation you would like to change, and use it in this and other exercises in this workbook.

The change I want to undertake is:**

....

....

....

....

example

An example of a change for my local authority might be:

- to increase how safe the community feels over the next five years (an outcome).

This might require changes in our services (outputs), in partnership working, in organisational structures, systems and culture (processes).

Taking one aspect of this as an illustration: we might need to change the culture of the highways engineers department so that they view their role and assess their activities by their contribution to community safety.

Measures of overall success might include: a drop in the reported fear of crime and in road traffic accidents.

Assessing the success of culture change in the highways department might involve assessing the nature of their strategies, the extent of user involvement, and feedback from the public and from partner organisations.

....

....

....

....

....

....

....

....

....

....

....

....

....

....

....

....

....

As a result of thinking about the change objectives for a particular project you might want to revisit your own objectives for this workbook. (Exercise 1)

Different perspectives on change

Most organisational change books are written from the perspective of relatively senior managers who wish to introduce changes to some aspect of their organisations, such as to the culture, structures or work processes. These changes are then seen to have implications for others in the organisation whose reactions to the changes need to be managed.

To some extent, this workbook follows this approach. However:

- It is possible to use the approaches we outline even if you are in the middle of the organisation. For the purposes of this workbook, you can read 'the organisation' to mean your department or section, while everything outside your department may be seen as part of 'the external environment'.
- We offer some alternative frames of reference within which organisational change can be viewed.
- We ask you to consider the questions, 'Whose change is it anyway?' and 'If it is yours, what gives you the right to impose it on others?' The answer may be, 'I'm the boss' but, without a more deep-rooted sense of motivation, it will be hard to win the commitment that you need from others to make your change effective.
- We ask you, therefore, to think about the values which underpin the changes you want to make. What contribution will the change make to the needs of the organisation, those of other stakeholders and the general public good – i.e. to what we call 'social result'?

Exercise 3

Values and change

Revisit the change objectives you set in exercise 2 and take some time now to ensure that you are clear about the benefits of the change and who will gain from them. Make a list below.

What values are driving the change objectives and who will benefit from the change? Again make a list.

Are these the values that you believe should be driving the change and its direction? If not, which values should be doing so? We will return to see how these are reflected in practice as we move through the workbook.

Alternative ways of viewing organisations

Before we begin looking at change in more detail, it will be helpful to make explicit the mental models most of us have of the way organisations work.

The predominant view for much of the 20th century has been to see organisations as machines, which when they work well 'run like clockwork'. In this mindset, people are viewed as a largely homogeneous resource which can be organised and controlled with almost mechanical precision. According to such a model, organisational change is a matter of finding the right levers to pull and these would normally be in the hands of the people at the top of the structure.

In his book *Images of Organisations*[1], Gareth Morgan identifies eight metaphors or ways of picturing organisations, of which the machine is only one. The other seven are:

- **Organisations as organisms**: this views organisations as living systems within an environment. Key issues are adaptation to the environment and how to create healthy organisations.

- **Organisations as political systems**: what happens is the result of the pulling and tugging of political forces. Making things happen depends on accumulating enough political power, or recognising and using the direction of change being generated by the interplay of these forces. The nature of power and its sources will vary both within and between organisations. For example, within hospitals, consultants, nurses and other professional groups each have their own sources of power; these are somewhat different to those of councillors and officers within a local council.

- **Organisations as brains**: there has been increasing interest in the idea of organisations as processors of vast amounts of information and in the ability of organisations to 'learn', both characteristics of the human brain. Key questions would be how to design organisations that can learn and how to create a distributed intelligence that resides in all parts of the organisation.

- **Organisations as cultures**: the beliefs, assumptions, values and related patterns of behaviour have become increasingly of interest as a way of explaining what goes on in organisations and why some are successful and others not. Because of the importance of culture and cultural change, there is a section on this subject later in the workbook.

- **Organisations as psychic prisons**: this suggests that people and organisations get trapped in their view of reality and become incapable of seeing different perceptions of the world because that would be too threatening. This is used to explain how organisations which were once successful get overtaken by events, e.g. IBM in the 1980s. It also offers a good insight into why people find change threatening.

---

1. Morgan, G. *Images of Organisations* (2nd ed,) Sage, 1996

- **Organisations as flux and transformation**: this sees the world – and organisations – as naturally being in a state of constant change. This process creates the paradoxes and tensions that we experience in organisations.

- **Organisations as instruments of domination**: although we are usually presented with the idea that organisations are rational enterprises from which we all benefit, this may not be the whole story. They can also be used to pursue the selfish or sectional interests of a particular group, at the expense of others.

As Morgan points out, each view simultaneously helps to reveal and to hide some dimension of what happens in organisations. For example, the machine metaphor helps us see the purpose and interrelationships between parts of the organisation but it can blind us to the nature of the relationship between the organisation and the external environment.

In this workbook we draw upon a range of ways of looking at organisations but, inevitably, some predominate. For instance, we use the concept of the organisation as part of a 'whole system' a lot because it is particularly valuable in highlighting the relationship between an organisation and its external environment. The view of organisations as political systems also underpins our thinking: this is helpful in recognising that an organisation is not a 'unitary whole' but will include diverse interests, and that the realities of power have a significant impact on the choices that organisations make.

Exercise 4a

Making mindsets explicit – a metaphor for your organisation?

In considering how to bring about a planned change inside your organisation you will have taken a view (probably implicitly) about how your organisation works. It will be helpful to make this explicit. To do this, take a feature of your organisation – e.g. structures, approaches to training and development, or key jobs or tasks – and decide what metaphor would best fit your organisation as it is now. Is it like one of Morgan's? As well as summarising it in words in the space provided, try to draw a picture of it. (This will help you to make use of parts of your brain that may intuitively have built a picture of how the organisation works.)

....

....

....

....

....

....

....

....

....

....

....

....

....

....

....

An example

Contrasting approaches to change

To show how different views of the way organisations work may have a substantial impact on planning and introducing change, the following example contrasts the 'machine' and 'organism' metaphors in the case of the introduction of team briefing into an organisation.

Organisation as machine	Organisation as organism
• **Identify working groups and team leaders.** • **Identify who will brief whom down the line or 'cascade'.** • **Produce a timetable of briefing days.** • **Notify team leaders of their responsibilities and of the timetable.** • **Notify staff of the introduction of the system.** • **Begin the briefing process.**	• **Assess how individuals, teams and organisation will react to the proposed scheme.** • **Discuss with staff, managers or representatives the objectives of the scheme and how people can be helped to achieve what is required of them.** • **Run workshops to train people and 'grow' a scheme which fits.** • **Agree an implementation date and process.**

We have exaggerated the differences to make a point and, in practice, organisations would undertake activities from both columns, although some organisations do tend to be more on one side or the other.

Exercise 4b

Making mindsets explicit – a metaphor for your organisation?

What do you think is the predominant way of viewing your organisation amongst the people who work in it? What metaphor would they use to describe it?

....

....

....

....

Summarise how this view of your organisation accords with reality. What are its limitations? Does this provide any clues about why any past change initiatives have been unsuccessful? How might it affect how you approach change in future?

....

....

....

....

....

....

....

....

....

....

....

....

....

....

....

....

....

....

Why is change an issue?

The pace of change

'We need to recognise that there is no Lake Placid up ahead, where we can consolidate and catch up, but only more white water rapids from here on; in fact Niagara Falls may be just around the bend.'

– a senior manager

As the above quote suggests, we have reached a point where change has become the norm rather than the exception. There may be periods when the pace of change slows, and times when it picks up, but we should be working on the basis that change is something we are going to have to learn to live with.

Whatever the pace and immediate and underlying causes of change, for change management to be successful people need to:

- understand the external context within which the organisation is operating;
- have ways of analysing the current internal issues and responses to change; and
- identify those factors that are driving the change and those issues which may well hold back the change process.

Each of these is now explored in more detail.

The pressures for change

Much has been written about the general reasons why change has become endemic: the economic, social, political and technological drivers behind the pace of change in the late 20th century. It would not be appropriate here to examine in detail the current global forces for change, partly because this would date quite quickly.

Nevertheless, in thinking about what is driving change at any particular time, it can be helpful to categorise 'drivers for change' at a number of different levels.

Seismic shifts, as the name suggests, are the deep underlying forces which are having a global impact. Examples might include:

- **globalisation, regionalisation and localisation** – the paradox in which a lot of production is being planned on

a global basis by multinational companies, while 'regions' such as Scotland and the Basque Country pursue greater independence, and more emphasis is being placed on community involvement in local decision making;

- **the information economy** – turning information into commodities or products, such as seen in the emergence of the World Wide Web;
- **networked organisations** – increased connections between organisations, the 'softer' boundaries between them (e.g. those working jointly to tackle social exclusion), and the creation of 'virtual' organisations.

In *The Network Society*, Manuel Castells provides an in-depth discussion of these trends[1].

The Government's long-term agenda, currently referred to as 'the third way', provides a framework within which more specific policies are pursued. Key dimensions of this agenda include: fulfilling election pledges in order to secure a further term of office; reconstructing the relationship between the citizen and the state; demonstrating economic competence; and devolution. The emphasis is on:

- shaping outcomes
- reconfiguring services and working across boundaries
- no inalienable right of particular organisations to exist
- transparency
- multiple accountabilities
- evidence-based risk taking.

A wide range of policy initiatives 'bubble up' from this long-term agenda. If managers try to respond to each of these separate initiatives they easily become prey to 'initiative overload'. With an eye to the underlying long-term agenda, however, they can see that there are a relatively small number of key areas for development. The wise manager will keep their eye on the papers, journals such as *Harvard Business Review* and *Management Today*, and use their networks both inside and outside of the organisation so that they can continue to spot longer-term external trends. This enables them to fashion an appropriate response, avoid overload and communicate to their staff the context that is influencing their thinking. This latter action is particularly important since the links between various change initiatives, if they exist at all, often reside only in the heads of senior managers.

1. Castells, M., *The Network Society*, Vol 1 of *The Information Age: Economy, Society and Culture*, Blackwell, 1996

Exercise 5

The context of change

From where do you gather your information about what is happening in the world that might affect what you and your organisation do?

....

....

....

....

With whom do you share and explore your ideas?

....

....

....

....

What are the main drivers of change to which you feel your organisation needs to respond over the next three years? Make a list below and then check it with colleagues.

....

....

....

....

....

....

What change initiatives are currently running in your organisation? How does the one you are planning fit with these?

....

....

....

....

....

....

....

....

The nature of change

For simplicity we talk in this book about 'a change' when, in practice, organisations are frequently faced with many simultaneous changes. However, as indicated above, often only a small number of core changes are needed, even in the most turbulent of environments. Also, people find it hard to focus on too wide a range of new initiatives. It is therefore both possible and advisable to create links between different initiatives so that staff see them as part of a coordinated response to a particular situation and can understand their own role in it.

Organisational responses to change

Sometimes it is easy to see a direct connection between what is happening in the wider world and how our organisations need to respond to this. For example, the election of a new government in the UK in 1997, committed to greater user involvement, has led many organisations to make internal changes in order to achieve the government's policy objectives.

However some of the choices that organisations make about how they are organised, and the subsequent way in which they reconfigure themselves, may have a less obvious direct connection with external pressures. The natural desire in most organisations to improve on their current performance has led to initiatives such as 'Investors in People' (IiP) and continuous improvement programmes. These initiatives often require planned organisational change and development to make them effective. For example, the introduction of performance management and communications systems are key to achieving IiP.

Whatever the immediate and underlying causes of change, it is important to be clear about what is driving change and what is an organisational response (and why it is appropriate). Many staff need help to make this distinction between external pressures for change – such as 'Best Value' – and the organisational response – e.g. the introduction of new systems of user involvement, new job responsibilities and performance management. A failure to make this clear and to discuss the forces that are shaping the organisation can leave staff believing that the actions of senior management amount to capricious gambling with their future.

Exercise 6

Understanding change

How well informed are your staff about the external forces driving change and their possible implications? What, if anything, do you need to do to ensure that they are adequately informed?

....

....

....

....

....

....

....

....

....

....

....

....

....

....

....

....

....

....

As we have noted above, there will usually be two types of forces affecting your desired future for your organisation. First, there is your experience of the present: the problems you currently experience and want to resolve. The second type follow from your vision of how your organisation could be better, or needs to be different, in response to what you see changing in the external environment. Examining these two sets of forces and creating plans to deal with them is part of the normal strategic processes of organisations; we say more about this in our workbook Managing Strategy.

Nevertheless, deciding what to change, where to start and what to make the priorities isn't always obvious. Even when a change is being imposed from outside, like 'Best Value', it will not always be clear what internal changes the organisation will need to make to achieve the desired outcome. More common still is the situation where the organisation is able to distinguish the outcomes, outputs or types of behaviour it wants to change, but finds it difficult to see beyond the symptoms to the underlying causes. Tools and techniques that you can use to examine and hopefully resolve these types of problems are explored in the next chapter.

An Overview of the Change Process

The preconditions for effective change

To create a strategy for organisational change, you first need to assess whether all the necessary conditions exist. We might express this in the following 'equation':

Change = Dissatisfaction with present x Vision of future x Practical first steps x Capability to implement

Change can occur *only* when all four of these elements are in place.

- *the absence of* **pressure for change** *causes* **projects to sit at the bottom of in-trays**

- *the absence of* **a clear, shared vision** *causes* **false starts that fizzle out**

- *the absence of* **the capacity for change** *causes* **anxiety and frustration**

- *the absence of* **first steps that lead to action** *causes* **haphazard efforts and false starts.**

Understanding the link between the causes and symptoms allows you to use this as a diagnostic tool. For example, finding that your change projects are sitting at the bottom of people's in-trays can be taken as a sign that staff aren't feeling enough pressure for change.

pressure for change	capacity for change
a clear shared vision	first steps that lead to action

What happens if one element is missing?

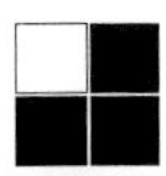 bottom of the in-tray

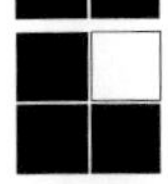 anxiety & frustration

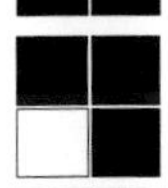 a fast start that fizzles out

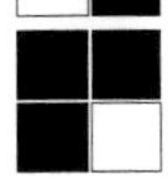 haphazard efforts & false starts

Exercise 7

Change requirements

Think about your own experience of change and check it against the criteria for change on the previous page. Do they give you any insights into why what you have done has worked or not?

Does the change project you are considering meet the four criteria or is it suffering from any of the symptoms?

Does it hurt too much?

All change activities involve some sort of cost to the people involved or to the organisation. A change project will succeed not only if all the elements are in place but also if, together, they are greater than the cost or effort involved.

Change, therefore, occurs when

dissatisfaction x vision x practical steps x capability > costs or effort or pain

As we will see, an important aspect of creating a change strategy is to give attention to both sides of this 'equation'. This will mean:

- building a constituency of understanding about current problems and the resulting dissatisfaction with the present;
- developing clear, attractive pictures of the future;
- clarifying how to get there;
- building the capacity to deliver the change; and
- minimising the perceived or anticipated cost (or pain) of change.

Our framework for change

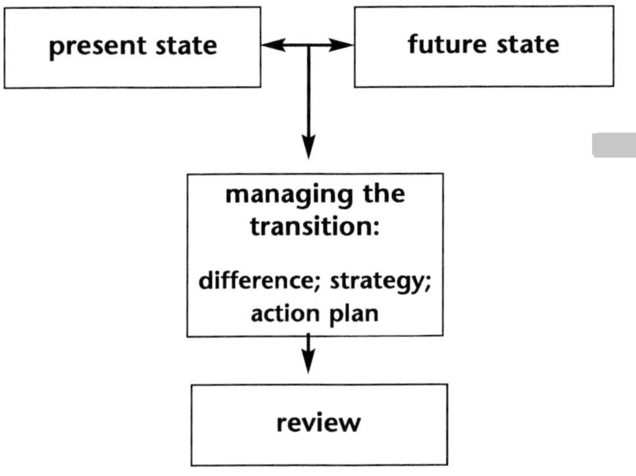

The rest of this workbook uses the following framework for achieving change:

1. **Assessing the present state of the organisation**. This means making a thorough analysis of what you have now, which is in some sense being identified as problematic.

2. **Imagining the desired future.** Developing a vision of how you want the organisation, or some part of it, to be.

3. **Managing the transition** between the present and the desired future. This involves:

   - identifying the key differences or 'the gap' between the present and the desired future;

   - developing a strategy to bridge the gap, including building individual and organisational capacity and sufficient support for the change;

   - developing an action plan for implementing the strategy, including first steps.

4. **Review.** Once the change is completed, then it will be important to review your progress, and to learn from what worked and what didn't.

The first two elements help us to clarify what needs to change; the third focuses on how to bring this about; and the last element enables us to learn from successes and failures.

This framework for organisational change has sometimes been criticised on the grounds that life has become a lot more complex than it allows for. When the external environment is in a turbulent state, it is far from easy to be sure about the present state of an organisation, let alone to define the future. Further, given the pace of change, many organisations are having to begin new, major change projects while existing ones are still under way. This calls for more iterative rather than linear approaches to change.

However these objections don't remove the need to have some way of addressing the key change issues, as this framework does. They do suggest that the framework and the tools associated with it should be used sensitively. For example:

- if organisations are living in permanent transition they need to put more effort into continuous learning

- if the more distant future is impossible to define then organisations can create a general sense of direction, take a small step, learn, and adjust as necessary.

To take account of these objections, we probably need to think differently about the future, and give more attention to learning from and managing the transition. We will explore this further as we consider planning for change in more detail. For the moment, you might like to think about what you have done in the past.

Exercise 8

Past change efforts

Where have you tended to put your change efforts in the past?

- ❑ assessing current problems
- ❑ visioning the desired future
- ❑ managing the transition
- ❑ reviewing progress/success/failures

Do you think you need to change the balance in the future?

....

....

....

....

....

....

....

....

....

....

....

....

....

....

Analysing the Present State

This chapter outlines four techniques that should help you focus on aspects of the current state of your organisation that you feel you need to change in the future.

1. Stakeholder analysis

Mapping the organisation's stakeholders and then assessing what they are currently 'saying' to you and what this is telling you about the current state of the relationship is a good way of ensuring that change plans are rooted in reality.

A stakeholder is any person or organisation who feels that ***they*** have a legitimate interest in how you perform. Draw a map (like the one below) that identifies who your stakeholders are, both inside and outside of your organisation, and shows which are the most influential. This analysis will help you to identify the kinds of changes you are likely to have to make.

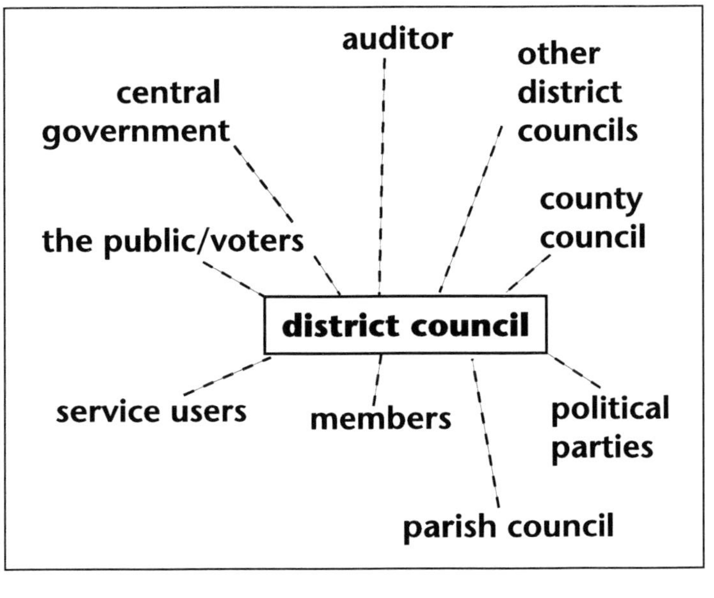

Having identified who your stakeholders are, you might review what their expectations are of you. For instance, what do they say they want? Does this match your experience of what they really want?

And what are your expectations of your stakeholders? Are they aware of your expectations?

How do you respond to each other's expectations? And what does this say about the present state of your relationship?

An example

Leisure service users:

1. They say: 'We want women-only swimming sessions.'

2. Our response: 'We'll look into it.'

3. Our expectations of them, perhaps as illustrated by this response: 'They'll make do with whatever we provide.'

4. Their response: to write and complain to the local paper.

5. Conclusions about the current relationship? Can we really say we have a partnership?

2. Cause and effect analysis

Change raises interconnected problems. This technique helps you to disentangle them by providing a graphic representation of the connections between different problems. By tracing the causes and effects of these interrelated problems it becomes easier to identify the most appropriate problem on which to work.

You start by making a current organisational problem into a statement and placing this at the centre of a sheet of paper, as shown oppostie.

In one direction (say the top of the paper) you then identify the **causes** of the problem, (there will probably be several). Once you have done this, repeat the process, identifying the causes of those problems. Continue until the problems are becoming generalised statements of the obvious.

In the other direction, work down from your original problem identifying the **effects** it is having. Again, repeat this process until the effects are what might be termed a 'doom scenario' in which the organisation's survival is threatened.

This will give you a map of connected problem statements and help you to determine the most appropriate level of intervention. This may allow you to alleviate problems without the costs of major change or at least get you to focus on the most appropriate problem. For example, in the case illustrated, it might have been possible to solve the problem by recruiting or training more staff to deal with queries. However pursuing this analysis might lead the organisation's management to redesign jobs and train supervisors in how to manage the work flow.

Deciding the most appropriate level at which to intervene is ultimately a question of judgement, but this and some of the other techniques used to analyse the present state of the organisation will help you make that judgement.

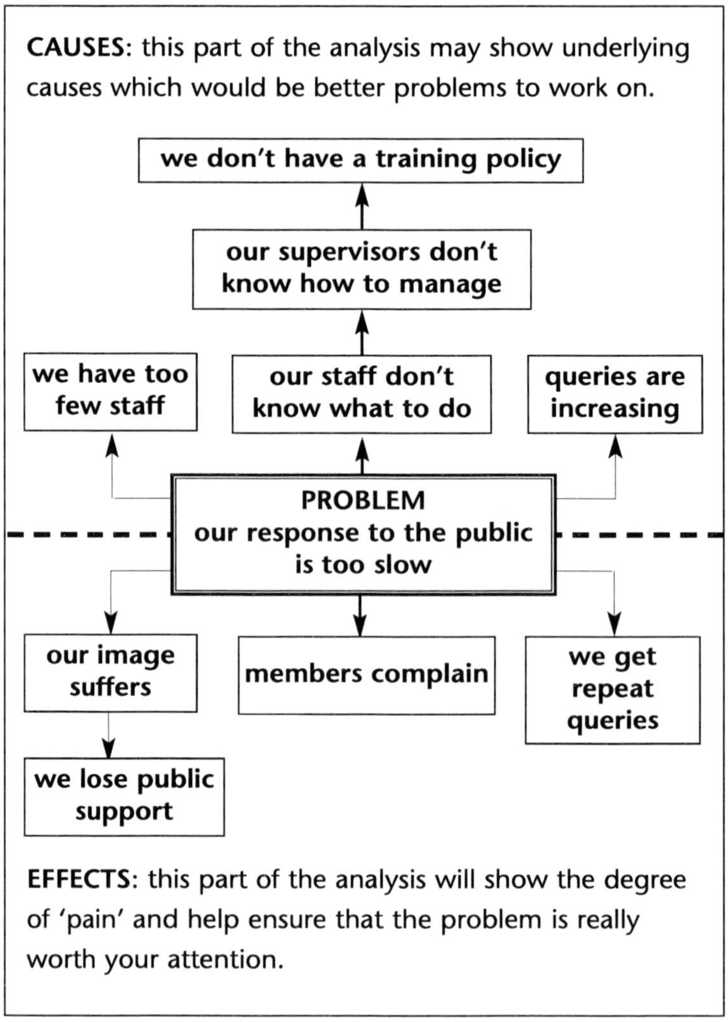

3. Organisational health check

In order to assess the current state of your organisation you need criteria for doing so. There are many different models of organisations but staying with the one by Jay Galbraith introduced in our book *Managing Strategy*, we would say that the main internal components or elements of the organisation are:

- **organisational purpose** and the current strategy for achieving it;
- **structure**: the formal hierarchy of reporting relationships, cross-organisational working, permanent and *ad hoc* teams and groups, and informal working structures;
- **work, tasks, roles and responsibilities**: what work is allocated to which posts; how people work, alone or in teams; whether people are given a 'complete' job or a part of one;
- **information and decision making**: communication and decision making methods and systems; who is involved and at what level;
- **reward systems**: formal and informal; financial and other rewards; what is rewarded;
- **human resource systems, policies and practices**: as they apply to such areas as recruitment, training, promotion, latitude to do the job;
- **organisational culture**: this will be expressed through all the above, especially the management style.

Because of its link to results, this model implies that your organisation is perfectly designed to achieve the results it is currently getting. If these are in some way unsatisfactory, then one or more of these elements needs rethinking.

The Healthy Organisation Checklist

- ☑ The organisation operates in a purposeful and goal-directed way.
- ☑ Our management structures have been designed around the needs of our service.
- ☑ Policy is well communicated throughout the organisation.
- ☑ Decisions are made by those close to where information is rather than based upon hierarchy.
- ☑ Our reward systems reflect achievement.
- ☑ Communication is relatively open; differences of opinion are valued.
- ☑ Teamwork across boundaries is encouraged.
- ☑ Conflict is managed (rather than suppressed or avoided).
- ☑ The organisation interacts effectively with the wider world.
- ☑ Work methods are improved through feedback and learning.
- ☑ People feel valued and part of the organisation.
- ☑ We give a good service to the people who call on us.

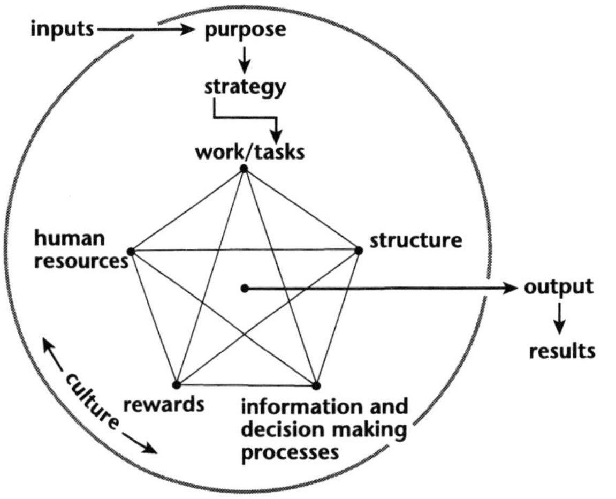

Organisational Design by Jay Galbraith

4. Priority problem listing

This technique simply involves specifying problems in the following format:

How do we...?

e.g. How do we reduce the time taken to respond to queries and applications?

These problem statements can then be listed in priority order. This will usually be helpful because there is rarely one discrete problem to be tackled. It is more likely to be the case that there are a whole constellation of problems requiring attention. These need to be identified and the connections between them made clear so that you can identify any priorities and/or potential domino effects, i.e. problems which if solved would have a knock-on, beneficial effect on other problems.

Summary of present state analysis techniques

All the above tools are helpful in identifying what works well and what problems may need attention. However it isn't possible to know everything, even about the present, and ultimately you are faced with making judgements, often on partial information, about priorities for change. The next exercise is designed to help you become more familiar with these tools but also to check out your judgement against that of your colleagues or others in your 'supporting cast'.

Exercise 9

Current problems

Practise using the above techniques for present state analysis to identify the key, priority problems faced by your organisation, or your part of it. Compare your analysis with that of your colleagues and, if they are different, discuss what different judgements you and they are making.

Looking to the Desired Future State

Introduction

Bearing in mind the external environment, what type of organisational future do you want to create? The following techniques should help you to decide this. But bear in mind that the future will always remain unpredictable and any sizeable, long-term change initiative needs to be able to accommodate and adjust to whatever happens along the way.

Thinking about the desired future raises the fundamental question of whose future this is and whose commitment to it is necessary. For simplicity's sake, this workbook is written as though you, the reader, are central to what is to happen. In real life, of course, other people are likely to be involved, from a very early stage, in debating and making decisions about the future. In any case, this is often a much better approach than trying to 'sell' your changes to others who have had no immediate involvement in deciding them. We will examine some of the methods for involving large groups of stakeholders in the chapter 'Approaches to changing organisations' and return to the critical decision of who to involve, and when to involve them, when we look at strategies for achieving organisational change. In the meantime, bear in mind that any of the techniques described in this section can be undertaken with a wider group.

1. 'Visioning' the ideal future

It can be too easy to allow our thinking to become trapped in the way we presently do things. Try thinking outside of the limitations of the present. One way to do this is to put what is generally believed to be practical to one side and imagine instead what your ideal world would be like. Techniques you can use to do this might include:

- **brainstorming**
- **'creative thinking' techniques,** such as drawing, drama or relaxation, that help you use different parts of your brain
- **proposing the opposite** – not because this will give you 'an answer' but because it might open up new possibilities. In his book *Creativity* Edward de Bono makes many suggestions about how to build your capacity to think creatively. It was, he says, because somebody asked the apparently ridiculous question, 'Why can't planes land upside down?' that a major re-thinking of cockpit design came about.
- **challenging 'mental maps'** or current practices. For example, ask yourself: 'What is impossible to do right now that – if you *could* do it – would fundamentally change the sector in which you operate?' Some recent examples include the belief that budgets had to be annual, or that consistently poor performers couldn't be dismissed, or that different public sector bodies couldn't share budgets.

Exercise 10

My ideal future

Use one or more of the above methods to generate a picture of your ideal future. Summarise its key features below. You could include such areas as:

- how you are seen
- the services or products you are delivering to whom
- what other key stakeholders are doing
- the culture, size and shape of your organisation.

....

....

....

....

....

....

....

....

....

....

....

....

....

....

....

....

....

Then use the techniques in the next chapter to sharpen your vision and agree the future you really want.

In *The Fifth Discipline* Peter Senge provides examples of the most common fallacious mental models and some ideas on how to uncover our own hidden or unconscious mental models.

Envisaging an ideal future would normally include some innovation. Peter Drucker[1] has famously warned us against seeing this as the province of the creative few. 'In innovation,' he says, 'as in any other endeavour, there is talent, ingenuity and knowledge. But ... what innovation requires is hard, focused, purposeful work.'

He sees most innovation as resulting from a conscious search for four internal and three external areas:

- **unexpected occurrences**, e.g. why a service turned out to be a tremendous success or an unqualified failure;
- **incongruities between processes for similar tasks**. The way in which we used to teach foreign languages, for instance, didn't utilise all the aids that each of us used to learn our mother tongue;
- **process needs**, e.g. advertisers needing to reach a public pay for free newspapers;
- **industry and market changes**. The arrival of the Internet, for instance, is creating many opportunities for new types of business and new ways of doing 'old' business such as home shopping;
- **demographic changes**, which are creating new needs for the care of both young and old people. Some local authorities are bringing these together in schemes such as 'adopt a granny';
- **changes in perceptions**. Despite improving health statistics, we are increasingly concerned about health issues. This is opening up new roles for public bodies in helping the public to assess and manage risk;
- **new knowledge**, which is the most obvious source of innovation, but it often takes years before someone finds a way of making this new knowledge useable.

To be innovative, to think differently about the future requires us to use both sides of the brain. 'Because innovation is both conceptual and perceptual, would-be innovators must also go out and look, ask and listen. Successful innovators use both the right and left sides of their brains. They look at figures. They look at people. They work out, analytically, what the innovation has to be to satisfy an opportunity. Then they go out and look at potential users, to study their expectations, their values and their needs.'[1]

1. Drucker, P. 'The Discipline of Innovation' in *Harvard Business Review* November-December 1998

2. Core purpose

It is worth revisiting your organisation's core purpose – i.e. what it is for – and asking whether this will still be appropriate in the future or, if not, how it needs to change. At this level, obviously, changes will be fundamental and will have a considerable impact. It has been suggested that much of the 'pain' experienced recently by people working in local government has arisen from a change in its core purpose.

What an organisation is for is not the same thing as what it does. The little boy who asked his father of Queen Victoria, 'Please, Daddy, what is that lady for?' goes to the heart of the role of the monarchy. We needn't explore that here, but you might like to consider how the core purpose of public bodies like local authorities has changed in the last decade. In the past, people would probably have said that local authorities were there to provide services to local people. Now they might answer that they are there to provide the means by which local people's voices can be heard. And in future they might say... ?

Exercise 11

Changing purpose

Has the core purpose of your organisation changed, or does it need to? Is this recognised? How would this affect what your organisation does? Make some notes here and then take a look at our brief summary (about local authorities) below.

....

....

....

....

....

....

....

....

....

....

....

....

....

....

....

....

example

The impact of a change in local authorities' core purpose

The change in local authorities' core purpose has clearly led to less emphasis on direct service delivery and is beginning to lead to changes in how local voices are heard. This includes everything from electoral arrangements, to polls on council tax, to user involvement in service design and delivery. In turn, these are leading to changes in priority activities, structures and jobs.

We don't know if local authorities will have a different purpose in future, and if so what it will be, but it might be along the lines of helping the public to understand and manage risks.

3. Scenario writing

Scenarios provide a rich picture of 'alternative futures' to which an organisation may need to respond. By thinking through what your responses would be to particular sets of imaginary circumstances, you may find that there are a lot of actions which it would be wise to set in hand, regardless of what the future actually brings.

The main steps involved in the technique of scenario writing are:

- identify a range of possible ways for things to turn out in the future
- write a scenario – a 'picture' – for each, or for a representative sample
- identify what you would be doing in each case if you want to achieve your purpose. On the basis of this, identify what needs to change now. This could involve any elements of organisational design or external relationships, outputs or results.
- decide which of your scenarios are desirable, and which are undesirable, and whether there is anything you should be building into your plans to help achieve one and avoid the other.

There is a more substantial section on scenarios in *Managing Strategy*[1], and a more detailed explanation of the technique, along with two future scenarios, in *The Future for Public Services: 2008*[2], published by the Public Management Foundation.

1. Tarplett, P. and Parston, G. *Managing Strategy*, Office for Public Management, London, 1998
2. Public Management Foundation *The Future for Public Services: 2008*, London, 1998

4. The future organisation

To give some attention to what your organisation will look like, use the model given in the section on present state analysis (see page 21). What do each of the elements need to be like and how will they fit together to deliver the outputs and results you want?

Exercise 12

Looking ahead

You started to do this in exercise 2 but you might like to use the above techniques to revisit and possibly sharpen your view of what the future state of the organisation needs to be.

....
....
....
....
....
....
....
....
....
....
....
....
....
....
....
....

Detailing the differences between present state and desired future

Assuming that you are now clear about the problems you want to tackle and the future state of the organisation you want to create, then the key differences between the present state and the state you desire may already be obvious to you. Nevertheless, it is worthwhile pulling them together and checking that you have identified all the key elements that need to change.

You could do this under the broad headings:

- core purpose
- outcomes: e.g. how you want to be perceived in the public domain; the results you want to achieve
- outputs: the services you produce for your users
- processes: the internal structures, systems, methods etc. you use
- inputs: the people and other resources you bring into the organisation to achieve your purpose.

Listing all these differences will help you to begin to think about the next stage of the work involved in bringing about the change(s) you want.

Exercise 13

Key differences

Compile a list of the key differences between the present state of your organisation and the future you desire. You could treat this as a group exercise, or you may prefer to do this on your own initially and then discuss your list with colleagues or other members of a group.

....

....

....

....

....

....

....

....

....

....

....

....

....

....

....

....

....

....

....

Approaches to Changing Organisations

Introduction

Once you have decided what you want to change, but before deciding on a strategy to achieve the change, you need to think about the methods that you might use to bring about organisational change and where you are going to concentrate your efforts. This chapter is going to look at methods, and we have categorised them into four main types: those aimed at the individual; those that can be applied to groups or teams; those that are used on an organisation-wide level and, finally, methods that are aimed at changing the 'whole system'.

1. The individual

Many organisational change efforts seek to achieve their goal by targeting individual activities and behaviour. The argument goes: since the organisation is made up of individuals, if you change their behaviour this will effect a change in the organisation. Some typical techniques include:

1. **Giving information**, about the need for change and what is required in the future. This is useful but limited, since downward communication from management to staff does not do much to encourage support, involvement or commitment to the future on the part of employees.

2. **Training**. Providing individuals with the skills and/or attitudes required for the future. This may be necessary but is unlikely to be sufficient. Attitudes and the willingness to use new skills depend at least as much on the work setting as they do on an individual's behavioural predispositions.

3. **Counselling**. Tackling deep-rooted behaviour through counselling is more effective than training but is unlikely to bring about organisational change. However, failure to deal with inappropriate behaviour, particularly amongst those in key positions, is likely to undermine change efforts.

4. **Selection for jobs**. The recruitment of new staff, particularly at senior level, can be a key contributor to change, as they bring new skills and approaches. Who is appointed/promoted and their behaviour afterwards also sends important messages to other staff about the direction of the organisation. However it is all too easy for most new appointees to be pulled into the existing organisational culture.

5. **Termination**. Used selectively this can be a powerful tool, taking power away from those who would inhibit change and sending a message through the organisation. Ricardo Semeler describes having to do exactly this when taking over the business from his father.[1]

1. Semeler, Ricardo, *Maverick!*, Century, London, 1993

6. **Behaviour modification**. This involves trying to change people's behaviour through the application of rewards and sanctions. Performance related pay, against identified personal objectives, is one example. These approaches can have good short-term results but many organisations are now choosing to reject them: it is difficult to specify what is to be rewarded and to measure whether it has been achieved but, more fundamentally, few individuals achieve their results through their own efforts alone.

Individual approaches to organisational change may well have a supporting role to play but, on their own, they usually fail. This is because they take inadequate account of the extent to which individual behaviour is set by the organisational and group context.

Exercise 14

Individual-based approaches

Outline any experience you have had of the above types of approaches, identifying what worked and what didn't. If possible, discuss these with colleagues and try to reach a consensus about the usefulness of these techniques.

2. Group-based approaches

Some people have sought to overcome the difficulties inherent in individual approaches by working instead with groups or teams. Many of the same approaches can be taken, but delivered and discussed in work groups or teams. For example:

- giving information to work groups
- providing skills or behavioural training to work groups
- team building, based on themes like:
  - purpose and strategy, to give a clearer sense of direction and to ensure time is given to the 'right' things;
  - procedures and systems to ensure things are done correctly;
  - roles and responsibilities to clarify who will do what, and to ensure there is a good 'fit' between roles;
  - the skills needed to work well in a team;
  - values and types of behaviour as a basis for changing how people work together in and across their work groups; i.e. group dynamics.

They may also be used within wider organisation-based approaches such as the introduction of self-managed teams as part of changes to structure and decision-making authority, or as part of work redesign from individual to group tasks and rewards.

Exercise 15

The whole group

Write a brief summary of your experience of group-based methods of change. When do you think they are most helpful?

....

....

....

....

....

....

....

....

....

....

....

....

....

....

....

....

....

Like the individual approaches, group-based approaches can be useful in supporting change, particularly if they cover the whole or a large part of the organisation. If carried out piecemeal, however, they tend to suffer from the same problems as individual-based approaches, i.e. they are lost within the organisation's existing systems and culture.

3. Organisation-wide approaches

Introduction

You will want to change your organisation, or some aspect of it, because you believe that it is not producing acceptable results – results that either help people, or serve people's needs, or fit with the pace of change in the external environment.

We have already seen that you can do much to change your organisation by working with the people in it, either individually (by sacking poor performers, employing better people, training or counselling the people you have) or as teams or groups which interact with each other (by team building, re-organising the teams or improving team management).

But people are only one part of the complex web of elements that make up an organisation – and there's not much mileage in changing the people unless you are confident that all the other elements are in good shape and working together well. Good people in good teams are still not much use without a suitable structure, decision making authority and adequate information.

The framework illustrated here should help you to explore the various interrelated elements that make up your organisation, and to see how they fit together.

What can be changed?

Returning to the model of organisation design we have already used, you'll recall that, by definition, it is 'perfect' for the results you are currently getting. To change these results, you need to change some aspect of the design. Bear in mind that – as the diagram illustrates – they are all interconnected, so it is important always to check how changing one aspect will affect the others.

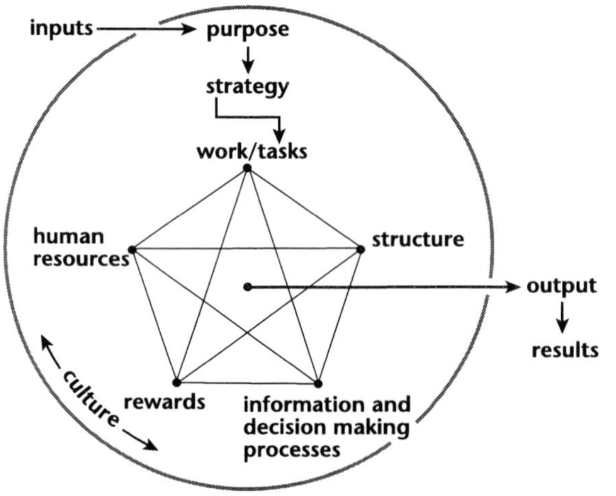

Using this framework, approaches to change could involve engaging key individuals or groups in rethinking:

- the core **purpose** of the organisation and the strategy by which it is to be achieved;
- the nature of the **work** or **tasks** people in your organisation perform;
- **structure**: reporting relationships, cross-organisational working, permanent and ad hoc teams and groups, and informal working structures;
- the authority to make **decisions**, the methods by which decisions are made

and **information** communicated, what is communicated to whom, and when to facilitate this;

- what is **rewarded**, why and how, and what sanctions the organisation imposes;
- **human resources**: who is recruited, promoted, 'let go', the skills or competencies required and how they are developed; and
- how all of the above fit together.

To assess how well the elements fit together, we need to assess each pair of elements in turn. We have given some examples of this below.

Organisational culture

A common place for people to focus their efforts when they want to bring about change is that of the organisation's 'culture'. One reason for choosing culture is that it is such a powerful factor both within the organisation and in how it deals with the outside world.

Some organisational cultures are characterised by their considerable resistance to change. These days, recognising that a state of change is likely to be the norm rather than an exception, many organisations are keen to change this state of affairs and to encourage a culture that explicitly sets out to facilitate change.

example

Testing how well it all fits

Pair of elements	An assessment
Human resources *and* tasks	e.g. how appropriate are the people we recruit for the tasks/roles they must carry out? Are the jobs well designed so they attract the people we need?
Tasks *and* structure	e.g. do reporting relationships support people in carrying out their tasks?
Tasks *and* rewards	e.g. does the reward system lead to the appropriate recognition of those who perform tasks the way we want them to?
Information/decision making *and* structure	e.g. does structure facilitate flows of information and authority to make decisions at the level we want?
Structure *and* rewards	e.g. does the structure facilitate career progression?
Rewards *and* information/decision making	e.g. do people get feedback on their performance?
Tasks *and* information/decision making	e.g. do people have the information and decision making authority to complete tasks?
Structure *and* human resources	e.g. do we have the skills needed throughout the structure?
Human resources *and* rewards	e.g. is the behaviour we want to encourage being rewarded?
Human resources *and* information/decision making	e.g. is authority matched by ability?

An organisation's culture can work at number of different levels:

- **the outward signs**. On the surface, culture is visible in mission statements, logos, rituals, symbols, espoused values and so on;
- **ways of working**. Underneath the outer manifestations, culture includes the collective ways of thinking and behaving, the way things are done, and the unwritten rules and norms;
- **feelings and emotions**: the ground from which outward signs and ways of working spring. They include how things feel, the emotional climate, and are often illustrated by the stories and myths which are passed on within the organisation.

Whether an organisation's culture is weak or strong – or diverse – it is generally difficult to change: to do so will require a sustained effort over a long period. This is hardly surprising since the culture will have grown over a long period and will be embedded into the organisation in many ways. The 'formal' carriers of culture can be seen in aspects of the organisation such as the way information is communicated, and these can be changed. But the 'informal' carriers, and those which reside at a deep level in the organisation – the stories and myths – will take far longer to move. They are often a reflection of how senior figures have behaved, and continue to behave, rather than what they espouse. An effort to change the culture will therefore need to be supported by the behaviour of senior figures in the organisation.

Given the power of stories, one way of changing the culture therefore is to share powerful 'alternative' stories. The use of stories is an effective way of building understanding and the capacity for change.[1]

Changing culture may also involve targeting the three levels we talked about above – outward signs, ways of working and feelings and emotions – as well as the formal elements of organisational design. A good place to start is to gather some information about the existing culture. Using those three levels, you could undertake an audit that describes how things are now, and lists those aspects that you want to keep, to discard and to create.

The use of questionnaires/surveys and focus groups are particularly helpful for gleaning a broad cross-section of opinion both about the existing culture as people perceive it and the culture that people believe would be desirable. It may be helpful to ask 'outsiders' such as service users or new arrivals in the organisation who will see it with fresh eyes.

Any of these approaches will help to unearth the symbols and stories that illustrate the deep culture that needs to be tackled. Interactive approaches to data gathering such as these have the extra important benefit of involving people in the process of change from an early point.

An approach to culture change favoured by many organisations has been to work with staff to define values

1. see for instance, Shaw, G., Brown, R., and Bromley, P., 'How 3M is Rewriting Business Planning' in *Harvard Business Review*, May-June 1998

and to use these to write statements about competencies or behaviour which can then form the basis of self-assessment, feedback from colleagues and development plans. If these statements about desired behaviour can in some way be linked to rewards, then people are more likely to believe that they really are important. This can easily form part of a performance management system, as shown in the diagram below.

Less formally, individual managers can help create the culture they want by clarifying and publicising what they will value and reward and what they will not tolerate and the sanctions they will impose. This is using the power of sharing expectations with colleagues and of getting and giving feedback.

As we have noted, a good place to start in any culture change effort is with an assessment of the present culture. The next exercise, 'Creating your own culture', gives you the chance to do this for your organisation, using the techniques described in this section, as a starting point for thinking about the changes you want to make and how to go about them.

Exercise 16

Creating your own culture

Try this for yourself using this framework (the rewards and sanctions should be within your control and not just pay and promotion or discipline and dismissal).

I will value:

....

....

....

....

....

The rewards:

....

....

....

....

I will not tolerate:

....

....

....

....

Sanctions:

....

....

....

....

Exercise 17

Culture and change

Undertake an assessment of your organisation's culture. How would you describe it at the different levels of:

a) the outward signs? ....

b) ways of working? ....

c) feelings and emotions? ....

How does it need to be in order to help you achieve the results you want?

For example, taking the case of the highways engineers department (page 6), to make it the way they want it to be, the following changes might be identified:

a) the outward signs – mission statement needs to mention our contribution to the well-being of the community
b) ways of working – lighting replacement should be arranged around needs, not schedules
c) feelings and emotions – stories and deep beliefs about the importance of working with (rather than 'doing to') local communities.

....

You may find, in practice, that a good place to start is by rethinking espoused values and introducing re-defined roles, responsibilities and authority to act. Changes to feelings and emotions can then be left to 'catch up' with the new reality.

Exercise 18

My 'new' culture

Describe how you want your new culture to be and put down your first thoughts on how you might start to bring it about.

....

Exercise 19

Organisational design

a) Think about and then discuss with your colleagues which aspects of organisational design (strategy, structure, work design, communications, decision making, rewards and sanctions, human resource policies and practices, culture) you have had experience of changing. How effective were the changes?

....

....

....

....

....

....

....

....

....

....

....

b) Which will be most suitable for the changes you have in mind and what should be in the lead?

....

....

....

....

....

....

....

....

....

Where do I start?

The problem with organisation-wide approaches is that they are potentially so big it is sometimes difficult to know where to start. There is no pat answer to this because it largely depends on your earlier analysis of current problems and where you want to get to. Put another way, wherever you begin, the changes should be driven by your core purpose and strategy to achieve it. Form should follow function.

Many organisations decide to start with structure – because it is easy to redraw organisational charts – but they often ignore important supporting changes in responsibilities, decisionmaking authority and communication. In fact, there are many arguments against structure-led change: it is unsettling for many staff, it doesn't address the purpose of the organisation and it has little impact on performance. This suggests that it would often be better to change structure last of all, when everything else is in place.

At the beginning of this workbook we looked at the mental models or metaphors people have for their organisations. Since these are nearly always implicit, a good first step is often to uncover these and get them out into the open. The key to planning effective change may be to start by changing how you and others think about the organisation. Wherever you start, you need to develop a strategy for introducing change and to ensure that you have the levels of commitment you need. Some guidance on how to do this is given in the next section.

4. 'Whole system' approaches

Introduction

If you want to change organisations – or the outputs delivered and outcomes achieved by one or more organisations – the final category of approaches are those that treat them and the other stakeholders that affect them as a 'whole system'. The following methods and techniques provide an introduction to different ways to do this. First, though, you need to define your 'system'. This is a key step and will have a significant impact on what follows.

As we noted earlier, it is possible to define the system as your part of the organisation, with everything else treated as the external environment. The benefit of this is that it highlights what is within your direct control and what you can only hope to influence or accept. At the other extreme, you could identify an enormous range of individuals, groups, other public and private sector organisations which have a legitimate interest in your outputs and outcomes. But it would probably be impractical to involve all these stakeholders in thinking about the change you are pursuing.

A more practical approach is to identify the range of stakeholders who will have a significant impact on the outcomes you want to achieve. This will obviously include people within your organisation, but may also include others such as partner organisations, other people who wield 'political' power, members of the public and perhaps the media. Focusing your 'system' in this way will enable you to make the best use of resources – by not going any wider than you need to, but nevertheless including all the key parties who must be involved for change to occur. This is sometimes called the 'critical mass'.

Having made your judgement about where to define the boundaries of the system, the next step is to get your 'critical mass' together to work on your proposed change. This may be done at what is termed a 'whole system event'.

As many kinds as the events themselves

Whole system events have been used since the late 1950s but the majority have happened within the last ten years. While it could be said that there are as many kinds of whole system events as there have been events themselves, it is possible to categorise the main types.[1] For the purpose of this workbook, we will look at the four most well-known: open simulations, 'future search conferences', 'open negotiation conferences' and 'open space technology'.[2] What they all have in common is that, in working on plans for change, they involve as wide a representation as possible of the stakeholders who make up the 'whole system'.

---

1. The authors are grateful to Jon Harvey at the Office for Public Management whose booklet, *Results Through Partnership*, supplied the information for this section.

2. *Large Group Interventions* by Bunker and Allen provides a good summary of whole system events.

a) Open simulations

Simulations are large events that are designed to help an organisation, or group of organisations, and their wider set of stakeholders to deal with the issues that will be confronting them as they approach a period of major change. A typical simulation would bring 40 or more people together for one or two days, and look at what is likely to happen over the course of the next few years.

In traditional management simulations, the designer decides in advance what the outcomes will be and then allows participants to 'discover' these as they act out pre-defined roles during the course of the event. We would term this a 'closed' simulation.

By contrast, in an 'open' simulation we present the participants with a hypothetical but realistic scenario and ask them to negotiate with each other to reach what each sees as the most desirable outcome. Participants enact a role that is similar to their own (but is not the same, since this is a simulated context) and make operational decisions in the face of 'events' and other factors that emerge during the simulation.

At key stages, the participants are asked to drop their roles and discuss what has happened and its relevance in the real world of their organisations.

Simulations seek to understand and harness the micropolitics of the system so that changes can be implemented as smoothly as possible. Each simulation is unique, designed to enable an organisation to 'learn from the future' by creating a fictional but realistic context within which new or emerging policies can be tested. They work best when significant changes to policies, structures or service delivery arrangements are planned and people want to learn more about what might happen before it actually does. For example, prior to the introduction of the internal market in the NHS, the Office for Public Management designed a simulation to help a regional office to work through the details of what this change might mean in practice. And, at the time of major reorganisation in local government, a simulation helped new 'shadow councillors' to practise their forthcoming roles.

The Office has published several reports of open simulations. See, for instance, *Mapping the Maze* (1997), *HealthMetro* (1997) and *Managing Beyond Gender* (1995)

b) 'Future search' conferences

'Future search' conferences were designed by Marvin Weisbord and have been developed by him and Sandra Janoff.[1] The approach has been made very accessible through a series of helpful manuals and case studies.

A future search conference usually has around 60 to 70 participants who, over the course of three days, aim to reach agreement over future directions. The process begins with an exploration of the past and then moves on to an analysis of the present. The conference participants then 'envision' the future that they wish to create for themselves before ending with a whole system agreement about what elements of the future they are all prepared to agree and work towards achieving. The future search conference has a fairly prescriptive model to follow, although a steering group decides the final agenda.

Future search is a process which is resolutely focused on finding the common ground that the whole system can agree on; whilst disagreements are acknowledged, they are not 'worked' in the way that they are in other processes (see 'open negotiation conferences', below). As with most whole system events, a future search requires commitment from the leading and most resource-rich stakeholders to see the process through. It is not wise, however, to undertake a future search conference unless you are sure you can plan, market it to stakeholders and resource it adequately.

1. see Weisbord, M., *Productive Workplaces: Organising and Managing for Dignity, Meaning and Community*, Jossey Bass, 1987

c) Open negotiation conferences

The basic idea of an 'open negotiation' conference is to create an occasion when the set of key stakeholders concerned with an organisation can assemble to negotiate and resolve a series of 'blocking' issues. The focus of the event, therefore, is on problems; by exchanging objective information and subjective perspectives, participants aim to arrive at an agreement on how to resolve these problems.

Generally, open negotiations work best over two or three days, with a gap before the last day. During the event, the stakeholders meet with each other, in pairs or groups. Agreements made are recorded and announced towards the end of the event.

Open negotiations work best when a number of difficult (and sometimes long-lasting) blockages are hindering progress and where past attempts to resolve these have not been successful. The events are also very useful when getting people together has proved elusive in the past and only a big event will persuade people to come. The process also prevents the endless 'looping' of bilateral negotiations that can be characteristic of 'stuck' organisations.

As with simulations, open negotiation conferences rely upon carefully collated data about the circumstances in question as well as the negotiating positions of the stakeholders involved. A future search (and an 'open space' – see below), on the other hand, whilst requiring careful preparation, use only the information that people bring with them to the event.

d) 'Open space technology'

'Open space technology' was developed by Harrison Owen.[1] He says the idea arose after a conference, the best bits of which, he felt, had been the coffee breaks during which the participants had networked and exchanged ideas within a wide range of people. He resolved to create a conference process that was, in essence, one long coffee break!

An open space conference begins with all the participants sitting in a large circle. A skilled facilitator invites participants each to suggest an issue (or more than one) that they feel passionate about and which they would like to discuss with others. These are listed on a flipchart until people run out of ideas. The facilitator then uses the list to compile a 'flexible timetable' of meetings over the two or three days of the event, such that it will be possible for everyone to attend as many meetings as possible in which they are interested.

These meetings are held (and may lead to further meetings), decisions are made, information is recorded and exchanged and, all in all, a great deal of work is achieved. Participants have often commented that, using this approach, they can sometimes achieve in a few hours work that would normally have taken months.

'Open space technology' is ideal when the various interests of different groups are largely unknown and there is a great need to forge connections between key stakeholders. Open space allows themes and issues of common interest to emerge in a wholly bottom-up way.

1. Owen, Harrison, *Open Space Technology: a user's guide*, Potomac, MD: Abbott, 1992

Exercise 20

Change targets and methods

First, review the work you did in exercise 13 on 'key differences' and update it in the light of any new understanding you have about what you will need to change in your organisation.

Thinking either of your organisation in general, or of the change project you identified earlier, which of the individual, group, organisation and whole system approaches will be most suitable to bring about the changes you believe need to be made?

Have you been involved in any 'whole system' events? If so, do you think the experience helped with planning change in ways that other approaches might not have achieved?

Creating a Strategy for Change

We have now spent some time looking at identifying present problems, building the vision of the future, and some of the methods we can use to involve individuals, groups and the organisation as a whole. We now need to consider how to build readiness and capability for change and then move to action planning. Most of the costs and pain of change are in the transition and this is also dealt with a little later.

1. Getting people ready for change

One way to create pressure for change is to raise people's awareness of current problems and the dangers they pose to the health of the organisation and those in it. Some of the work you did in 'present state analysis' will be helpful here. Unfortunately, one of the paradoxes of change is that when it is most needed it is hardest to achieve and, conversely, when you are best placed to do it, the pressure to do so will probably be at its weakest. This is illustrated in the diagrams.

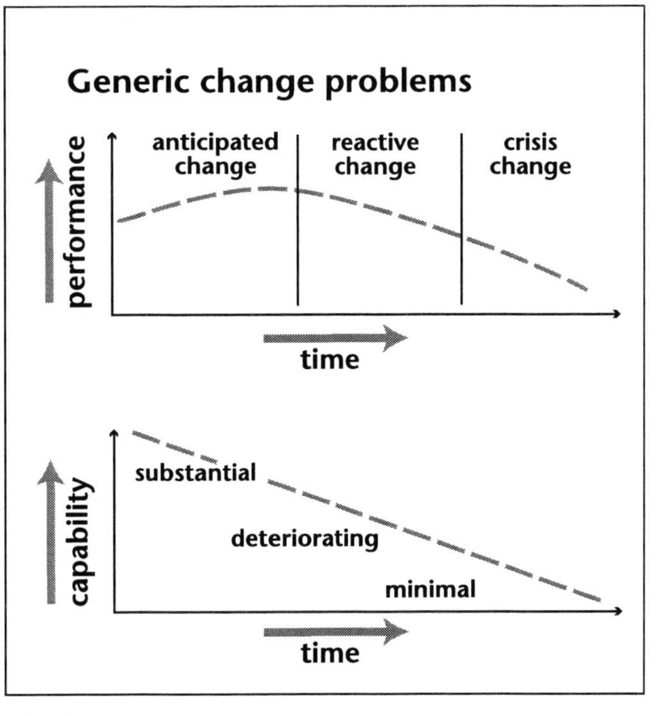

Substantial capability exists if you anticipate change but relatively little in a crisis. Unfortunately it is much harder to persuade people to change in anticipation of the need to do so because the issues are unclear and the pressures to change are low. This is shown in the table overleaf.

The tables below – illustrating typical or generic issues and how to plan to meet them – should help you to diagnose where you are and what type of approaches are most likely to work for you.

For example, if the management readiness is low, issues obscure and pressure to change low, you are probably anticipating changes that will be needed in the future. In such circumstances you won't find much enthusiasm for making cuts, externalising services or large scale development programmes.

illustration

Generic or typical change problem characteristics

	Change category		
	anticipated	**reactive**	**crisis**
Clarity of the issues	- obscure	- blurred	- sharp
Pressure to act	- low	- moderate	- high
Early obstacles	- problem definition - management readiness - credibility of the initiator	- selecting a response - management resistance - power of the initiator	- external credibility - depleted resources

As the pressure to change increases, the issues which need to be tackled become clearer but the resources to deliver it are reduced. Inevitably this affects what you may consider an appropriate strategy:

Generic implementation plans

	Change category		
	anticipated	**reactive**	**crisis**
Priorities: **– strategic** **– organisational**	 - reposition - raise awareness	 - revitalise - reduce resistance	 - retrench - find capability
Pace	- jog	- run	- sprint
Targets	- internal multiple	- internal 'pivotal groups'	- external and internal
Tactics	- many small steps	- avoid direct confrontation	- focused surgery

When the need to change is being anticipated, then the priority will be to raise awareness of external pressures and the possible responses. This may lead you to introduce a lot of small changes, such as changes to staff, systems or ways of working, as a way of preparing for more substantial change in the future. Organisations in crisis, though, will need to concentrate on building the capability to change. This may mean working with key groups inside and outside the organisation and possibly cutting some functions, or staff, out of the organisation.

You need, therefore, to think about your specific situation and what will work in your circumstances. The next exercise will help you to do this.

Exercise 21

Your own implementation plans

Where does the change you want to bring about in your organisation sit in terms of the above analysis: is it an anticipated, reactive or crisis change?

What are the implications of this for your change strategy? Try completing the table in the light of this analysis. For example, if you are in the crisis column, where might you start to build the capability, who are the main internal and external targets and what tactics might you think of using?

At what stage is my planned change?
(anticipated, reactive or crisis change) ....

How will this affect my implementation plans?

Priorities:

– strategic ....

....

– organisational ....

....

Pace ....

....

Targets ....

....

Tactics ....

....

Summary

You should now have a sense of how ready your organisation is to change and, given this starting point, will have developed some thoughts about how to move forward.

The more you are anticipating the need to change, the slower your pace and the more your efforts need to be directed at building awareness of the problems and threats. The closer you are to crisis, the greater the pressure and the clearer the need to change will be. Your efforts then will need to be aimed at building commitment to a particular way forward and the capability to deliver it, as quickly as possible. This may mean freeing up some key individuals from other tasks to provide the necessary capacity.

2. Assessing people's commitment

You need to determine whose commitment is necessary (individuals and/or groups), and at what level, for the change to happen. This group is the 'critical mass'. You can identify the critical mass by listing all interested parties (revisiting your earlier stakeholder analysis would be a good place to start) and assessing their readiness for change, their capability to change and their clout within the organisation, as shown in this partial example.

example

Who are my key stakeholders?

Individual (or group)	readiness H	readiness M	readiness L	capability H	capability M	capability L	clout H	clout M	clout L
chief executive	■			■			■		
director			■	■			■		
key individual	■					■			■
user representatives			■		■		■		

People scoring medium or high on these three dimensions are potentially the 'critical mass' necessary for your change. You can then analyse their present commitment – and the level you need it to be – using the following categories:

- they oppose the change
- they will let it happen
- they will support it
- they will make it happen.

This can be laid out in a chart like the one below.

example

How committed are they?

X = Present **0** = Desired

Individual (or group)	Oppose	Let	Support	Make
chief executive		0 - - -	- - - - - - - - - -	- - - X
director			X0	
key individual	X - - -	- - - - - - - - - -	- - - - 0	
user representatives		X - - -	- - - - - - - - - -	- - - - 0

Normally you will want to move people from left to right. However, in some cases, you might want someone to be less involved in creating change, asking them to 'let go' and simply let it happen (the chief executive in this example). You can undertake a similar analysis to assess whether people have the skills to fulfil their commitment to let, support or make change happen.

Exercise 22

Assessing what you have

For the proposed change you have chosen to focus on:

1. decide where you want to draw the boundaries of your 'system' (i.e. a sub-set of the organisation, the whole organisation, or the wider 'whole system')

2. use the techniques described above to assess:

- the key stakeholders
- the level of commitment you can expect of individuals and groups within the boundaries of your 'system'
- any gaps in people's skills that may reduce the effectiveness of your planned strategy.

....

....

....

....

....

....

....

....

....

....

....

....

....

....

3. Building capability – reducing resistance

Change will occur when the forces for it are greater than those against. A good way of building up your organisation's capability for the change you want to promote is to identify and then increase the factors which will help with that change while reducing those which will make it harder. One useful technique for doing this is 'force field analysis', a technique first described by Kurt Lewin[1], which is particularly useful when people's reactions and attitudes are affecting the process of change.

Generally speaking, it is easier and cheaper to reduce the resistance than it is to increase the force for change.

Exercise 23 explains force field analysis by outlining the steps you need to take. Two important points should be borne in mind when you undertake this analysis. First, define the desired change as explicitly as possible, so that you identify the ***actual*** forces at work, rather than the potential ones. Second, while you should certainly list and be aware of forces which lie beyond your control, don't expend your efforts over them; concentrate instead on those over which you ***do*** have some degree of influence.

1. see, for instance, Lewin, Kurt, *Resolving Social Conflicts: Field Theory in Social Science*, American Psychological Association, 1997

Exercise 23 a)

Force field analysis

Use this partially worked example and the outline on the opposite page to undertake your own force field analysis.

Example of a district council street lighting department which wants to increase its contribution to public safety.

Present situation:

people feel unsafe on the streets at night

helping forces

individual – You believe your department has a crucial role to play

interpersonal – You have good influencing skills and a good relationship with the CEO who is a supporter

group – There are some highly skilled people in your team

inter-group – There have been preliminary contacts with the police and the county council about 'joint working'

environmental – Government initiatives are encouraging user engagement

desired situation

increased feeling of well-being for the public

resisting forces

individual – You are new and relatively inexperienced

interpersonal – You have yet to build sound relationships with members of your team

group – Your team see their job as providing a 'professional service', rather than contributing to the organisation's 'mission'

inter-group – Most of the team prefer to work on their own or in the professional groups

environmental – Staff have historically not paid much attention to 'initiatives'

- actions to take ....

....

....

- most promising steps ....

....

....

- resources I'll need ....

....

....

Exercise 23 b)

Force field analysis

- Identify the change project or problem you want to work on. Do so in terms of a) the present situation and b) the future you desire.
- Make a list of the forces working for your desired change, and those working against it. These forces can be related to people, money and other resources, time, external factors, and so on – anything that can help or hinder you.
- Draw up a diagram from your list, putting helpful or 'driving' forces on one side and unhelpful or 'resisting' forces on the other and, wherever you can, identifying who controls the force.
- Estimate the relative strength of each force. An obvious way to do this is to draw the forces as arrows, using longer or fatter arrows for stronger forces.
- Identify those over which you have some control or influence and underline these.
- For each resisting force underlined, list the actions you could take to reduce or eliminate the force.
- For each helping force underlined, list the actions you could take to increase the force.
- Determine the most promising steps you could take toward making the change, and identify the resources that would help you to do so.
- Re-examine your steps and put them into a sequence, omitting any that do not seem to fit with your overall goals.

The partial example opposite can be used to guide you in undertaking your own force field analysis.

Were you facing a scenario like the one used in the example – and depending on the urgency of the change – you might want to spend time building relationships and winning the trust of key opinion formers in your team. You might construct a strategy to reduce resistance further by exposing staff to external realities, perhaps by bringing them into contact with users, exploring the implications of such government policies as 'Best Value', and discussing how you might respond as a a team. Given that each of us has our own particular responses to any proposed change, it will also be helpful to think about some of the more common individual reasons for resistance and how to manage them. We look at this next.

Overcoming individual resistance to change

Why do people resist change? It could be because of:

- individual self-interest, in which case you might help those concerned to see what new opportunities may exist in the new situation.

- individual styles. If you are familiar with the Myers Briggs Type Indicator you may recall that various 'types' react to change in different ways. Sensing Thinking Judging types (STJs), especially Introvert STJs, are thought to be particularly resistant to change because they have great respect for traditional approaches. But if they are convinced of a real threat to the organisation they can become powerful champions of change.[1]

- an emotional response. Again these vary between individuals, but the typical process that people go through is dealt with in the later section 'Change and the Individual'.

The change equation we used earlier is also useful for thinking about resistance.

Change occurs when

dissatisfaction x vision x practical steps x capability > costs or effort or pain

To support change, people have to be sufficiently dissatisfied with the present and attracted by the change for it to outweigh the cost, otherwise they will resist. You will need to think this through for each of the individuals who make up your 'critical mass'; each of them will have their own view of the change and a different level of resistance. (If, for example, a likely outcome of your proposed change is the demotion or redundancy of someone in this group, then they will probably resist very strongly.)

A lack of commitment, or resistance, to change indicates what might be termed a 'frozen' attitude and there are several methods we can use to 'unfreeze' these:

- problem finding/clarifying. Those concerned meet and discuss the issues in relatively unstructured groups, where the focus is on clarification, not action. These conditions help people to open their thinking to new ideas.

- educational interventions, to help people understand the issues.

- senior people setting an example, acting as role models and demonstrating desirable behaviour, helps to convince others that the change is important and has priority.

- rewarding desirable behaviour, which similarly sends a signal about what the organisation values.

1. Clancy, S., 'STJs and Change: Resistance, Reaction or Misunderstanding' in Fitzgerald, C. and Kirby L. (eds) *Developing Leaders*, Davies-Black Publishing, California, 1997

Commitment

You can build individuals' commitment to a change by:

- seeing the change from the other person's point of view and thinking through, from their perspective, how to make the change more attractive

- involving people in the change itself. This can be at one of three levels: they can be involved in shaping the decision – 'the what' – or in shaping its implementation – 'the how' – or in shaping the pace of change – 'the when'. But involving people in the change will require you to make careful judgements because, while increased involvement can reduce resistance, it can also provide more opportunities for opposition. This is likely to be the case if the people involved feel threatened by what is going to happen.

Exercise 24

Resistance and commitment

Use the techniques in this chapter to plan how you will overcome the resistance you anticipate and build the necessary commitment amongst the people who make up your 'critical mass'.

....

....

....

....

....

....

....

....

....

....

....

....

....

....

....

....

....

....

....

....

....

....

....

4. Rethinking 'resistance' – the micropolitics of change

The philosophy behind the previous section has been to see resistance as a problem to be overcome. This is based on the assumptions that those in favour of change are 'right' about the need for and direction of change and, more importantly, have or can build sufficient support to make it happen.

However, it is possible to see resistance in quite a different way. We might assume that all the stakeholders in an organisation have a legitimate interest in the outcome of any change and will use their power to influence what happens. In this case, the proponents of change are just one of these parties; the outcome will depend upon the interaction of the power of all the different stakeholders.

Taking this 'micropolitical' view of change would lead managers to assess the interests and responses of different stakeholders and to seek to use these to shape what actually happens. Strategies which also tap into broader organisational or deeper social, economic or political trends are likely to be particularly successful. For example, involving users in shaping service plans or service delivery is likely to build a powerful constituency for change, given the current political pressures on public sector organisations to move in this direction. (You might find it useful to revisit the earlier work on pressures for change to help you frame a change strategy which 'rides' these waves.)

Exercise 25

Using stakeholder and other pressures for change

Revisit your earlier stakeholder analysis and consider the attitudes of your stakeholders to your proposed change and the influence they can bring to bear.

Where might this lead your planned change?

How can you use your knowledge of stakeholder interests and wider change pressures to develop an effective change strategy?

5. Building the skills needed to support change

Your analysis may suggest that the skills of particular individuals and groups may need to be increased. This will involve training – which falls outside the scope of this workbook, although there are many training manuals available – and it will be important to include any such training or development in your planning.

Change and the Individual

Introduction

Thinking about individual responses to change will help you plan both how to prepare people for the change and how to manage them through the transition. It is easy to talk about change in general but it might make it more real to consider your personal experience and see what lessons can be learnt from it.

Exercise 26

Your personal experience of change

Outline a recent experience of change, perhaps in your work role or working relationships, or possibly a personal experience such as moving house. Try to recall what happened and how you felt about it. Did your feelings and reactions change over time? What help, if any, did you get to help you cope with the change?

....

....

....

....

....

....

....

....

....

....

....

....

Discuss your experience with others and see if you can identify any common patterns of feelings and reactions, as well as the factors which help people deal with change and those that hinder it.

1. Reactions to change

Obviously, individuals react differently, even to the same situation. It is possible, though, to identify some underlying principles. For instance, every change will involve:

- the loss of what existed before;
- the continuation of what is the same as before; and
- growth and the creation of new opportunities.

Depending on the circumstances, people will usually experience one or two of these much more strongly than the remainder. If someone is promoted, for instance, they are more likely to focus on the growth aspects, although they may also experience the loss of established relationships. If someone is made redundant, they are usually primarily concerned with the loss and will ignore what stays the same, e.g. their family and friends and the opportunities to do something new.

People's experience of loss has been likened to that of bereavement: we know that people will need to go through the same stages of grief when they lose their job as they do when they lose a loved one. These stages are:

- **Denial**: refusal to face reality. For example, staff served with redundancy notices often continue to work as normal. They may refuse to attend training or development courses, believing that, if they continue as normal, the world about them will be unchanged.
- **Anger**: this may be expressed at the situation, the person(s) seen as responsible, and possibly even by the individual at themselves.
- **Rationalisation**: an explaining away of what has happened. In the case of redundancy, for example, this might amount to saying: 'I was picked because my face didn't fit.'
- **Acceptance**: coming to terms with the reality of the situation.
- **Renewed action**: doing what is necessary to move on, e.g. revising CV, applying for jobs etc.

Do note, though, that these stages do not conform to a logical progression. It is possible for someone to get 'stuck' at an early stage or regress back to an earlier stage. Obviously, the passage of time helps people deal with their sense of loss but a recognition of the situation and support for the individuals concerned is helpful in speeding the process.

There are other similar frameworks used to explain how people experience what might be termed 'positive' change (such as gaining a promotion) and 'negative' change (such as being made redundant). They all show that change is never a 'straight line' progression from start to finish. Rather, it tends to conform to the following 'change curve'.

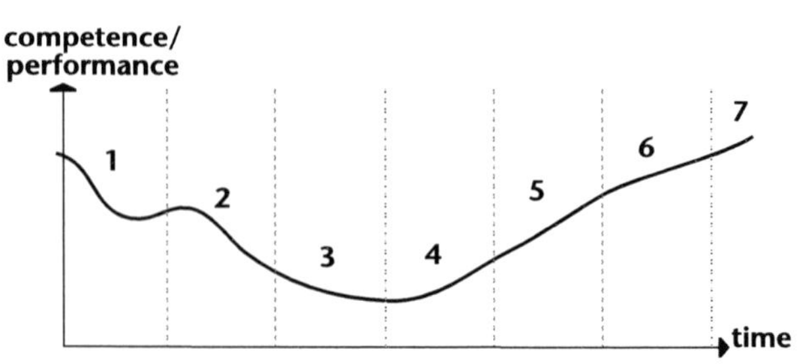

As you can see, this change curve relates competence or performance to time and has several stages.

1. **Shock and immobilisation**. Coming to terms with the reality of the situation can leave people feeling unable to act. This can be just as true when starting a new job as when being made redundant. Consequently competence and performance drop.

2. **Denial**. Denying the reality of the new situation but wanting to do something, people fall back on past behaviour and activities. This can lead to an improved performance - because at least something is being done - but it will generally be inappropriate to the new situation and this will start to become obvious.

3. **Frustration**. At this point people start to recognise the need to behave differently but don't yet know how. They may well see themselves, and be seen by others, as lacking competence.

4. **Acceptance**. Eventually we feel able to let go of the approaches that served us well in the past and to begin to experiment with new behaviour.

5. **Development**. If the process of change is successful, people start to develop and to become skilled in their new environment.

6. **Application**. In this phase people consolidate their identity in their new role and develop their own ideas about how things should be done. Relationships with others start to be resolved.

7. **Completion**. Feeling comfortable and competent once again.

It isn't possible to put a precise duration on each of these stages since this will depend on the individual and the circumstances. (Nevertheless, it has been estimated that it takes about two years for someone to feel competent in a new job.) Just as in dealing with loss, however, recognising that people go through these stages, and providing them with support, can help speed the process. Again, it is possible for people to fail to complete the process of transition demanded by the change. For example, instead of rising to the challenge of a new job they may stay in denial so that they end up doing their previous job (much to the irritation of the new incumbent!)

Exercise 27

Reactions to change

Does any of the above strike a chord for you, either in what you've experienced yourself or what you've observed others go through?

If so, what are the implications of this for how you manage change and the help you give people at the different stages of change? (Some thoughts are given on this overleaf).

viewpoint

Helping people through change

1. **Shock and immobilisation**: good listening and non-directive counselling helps people to clarify their thinking. Information (or advice on where to get it) is helpful but, because people find it hard to retain, it is best if this is written.

2. **Denial**: because the person is denying the reality of the change, it is impossible to discuss it with them. This is a good time to keep quiet, with perhaps occasional questions about what they want to achieve and how they might go about it.

3. **Frustration**: more listening and empathising is perhaps the best approach. It is important not to get into general moaning about how awful things are.

4. **Acceptance**: coaching, particularly non-directive coaching, will help the individual start to find their own solutions. You may need to give advice but if this is overdone it can be hard for the individual to find their own identity in their new situation.

5. **Development**: this is the stage when the range of development tools and approaches – e.g. coaching, training – become relevant.

6. **Application**: more coaching, encouraging and reinforcing learning will all help at this stage.

7. **Completion**: no specific help should be needed in relation to the change. In fact, the individual should now be in a position to help others.

2. Change and careers

The amount and unpredictability of change has made it hard for people to rely on the old certainties in their working lives. Even if they stay with one employer for a long time, it is unlikely that they will ever feel as secure as people normally did in the past. With organisations unable to give this security, it has become more important for staff to pay greater attention to their own career development and take a larger share of the responsibility for managing their own career.

It is unreasonable to expect people to take on this responsibility without any support from their employer. In any case, the employee is likely to feel that it is the employer who has broken the old 'psychological' or unwritten contract of 'work hard, do a reasonable job and you will be looked after'. It will probably be necessary, therefore, for the employer to take the lead in negotiating a new psychological contract. Whatever form this takes in a particular organisation, it is likely to be based on helping people to maintain their skills and stay employable, if not in that organisation then in another or in self-employment.

Managing the Transition

Responding to the pressures for change in a turbulent environment often raises dilemmas for managers. Examples of these include:

present	***vs***	**future**
kindness	***vs***	**efficiency**
urgent	***vs***	**important**
involvement	***vs***	**control**
improvement	***vs***	**demands**
risk	***vs***	**safety**

In the context of change management the following three dilemmas are particularly pressing:

1. **change *vs* stability**
   The organisation needs to continue to deliver the outputs, services, etc. for which it exists, while at the same time managing the change to a new situation. It is possible for senior managers to focus all their energy on the 'new' and emergent, and to forget that the organisation will only continue to survive if it maintains an appropriate level of service whilst it is going through the change process. In large-scale change it may be worth identifying 'anchors' which will stay the same throughout the change process and afterwards. This will provide some comfort to staff and help them to retain a focus on core activities and maintaining the organisation.

2. **external pressures *vs* organisational effectiveness**
   As we have noted previously, it is vital to respond to external pressures. However, if you try to respond to everything, you are likely to see your organisation disintegrate and possibly cease to exist. Your job is to filter what is coming in from outside and to find ways of making strategic choices about what to respond to.

3. **individual needs *vs* organisational needs**
   Each individual will have their own needs – economic, social, psychological, and so on – which may be different from or even conflict with those of the organisation. In this case, the organisation needs to find a way of maintaining the allegiance of enough of its members to achieve its purpose.

There are no pat answers to these dilemmas but, rather, balances that will have to be struck between these potentially competing forces.

Exercise 28

Dilemmas

In your chosen change initiative, which of the dilemmas described in this section are likely to be significant for you and your organisation?

Where will you strike the balance?

Looking at your organisation now, which of these dilemmas is most critical and how is it showing itself? What are the symptoms?

Are there any other dilemmas which are particularly significant for your organisation? If so, how are you managing them?

How people behave during transitions

In major change projects, changes to organisational arrangements may disrupt management control. Uncertainty can encourage political behaviour as people see power shifting but are not sure how things will turn out. Transition periods, in general, are characterised by:

- high uncertainty;
- perceived inconsistency;
- emotional stress;
- a feeling of a loss of control;
- people wanting past behaviour to be explicitly valued;
- increased conflict, especially between groups.

Managing through such a period, therefore, should focus on:

- good communication – providing clear information about the future, as far as is possible;
- being visible and proactive;
- valuing past contributions;
- giving time for people to disengage from the past/present;
- creating an awareness of the need to change.

Parts of the organisation that are not directly affected by the change will still need attention. The attitudes and anxieties of those who *are* affected won't be insulated within their departments.

Exercise 29

Transitions

Think about a change in which you were involved in the past.

How well was the transition managed?

....

....

....

....

....

....

What can you learn from this and the ideas in this section about how you would manage through a period of transition in the future?

....

....

....

....

....

....

....

....

....

....

....

....

....

....

If necessary, build this into your action plans.

Action Planning

If you have worked your way through the previous sections, you should now be in a position to plan what you need to do to achieve the change you want to bring about. Action planning is a whole subject in itself and we cannot even attempt to do it justice here. In brief, though, your action plan will need to have the following features.

- it must be related to the goals and priorities you have established for the change you want to bring about;
- it must be specific, rather than generalised;
- the parts of the plan should be integrated;
- the plan should be time-sequenced;
- the plan needs to be flexible and adaptable.

Your plan should include the changes to outcomes and outputs you want to achieve, as well as the internal changes, and the steps you need to take to get there. Most change efforts fail because they focus on the technical side of change and pay inadequate attention to its social aspects. Hopefully, the work you have done so far will have prepared you to build this aspect of change into your plan.

You also need to determine an appropriate management structure to ensure good leadership of the change project. This could mean: appointing a project manager; adding the project management role to that of an existing line manager; and/or creating a project management group consisting of interested parties, or a 'diagonal slice', or a group of 'natural' leaders, or a 'kitchen cabinet'.

However you decide to organise the leadership of your change project, the people who will be in leadership roles will need:

- the necessary authority (formal or informal) to mobilise the necessary resources;
- the respect of those with responsibility for continuing operations;
- good inter-personal skills, since a lot may have to be achieved without the use of formal line management authority.

The exercise overleaf should help you to draw up your own action plan.

Exercise 30

Action plan

My action plan to achieve the following change: ....

....

....

....

....

....

....

....

....

....

....

....

....

....

....

....

In drawing up your action plan, have you taken account of the following:

- the present state of the organisation?
- your 'mental maps' of your organisation, and those of others?
- your 'desired state' for the future of your organisation, and the social results you want to promote?
- people's reactions to change?
- the strategies, tools and techniques you might use?
- how you intend to manage the transition?

....

....

....

....

....

....

....

....

....

....

....

....

Review

Now that you have reached the end of this workbook, you might want to think about review at several levels and discuss these with your manager and other members of your 'supporting cast'.

1. In terms of your own personal objectives (exercise 1):

- did you achieve them?
- what were the most significant things you learned?

2. In terms of any particular change project you were working on:

- what worked well?
- what would you do differently next time?

3. What further learning needs has this workbook raised:

- for you?
- for others?
- for the organisation?

Good luck for the future.

Ordering further copies

To obtain further copies of this workbook or of other workbooks in the *Inside Managing for Social Result* series, please photocopy and complete this form and return it with your cheque, credit card details or organisation's purchase order to the address below.

Workbooks in the series *Inside Managing for Social Result* cost

£22.90 each, plus £1.20 p&p = £24.10

For orders of 10 or more copies a discount of 20% applies

= **£18.30** each, (plus postage of £6.00 for each 10 books)

Or you can buy all three books in the series at a 20% discount

£54.96 plus £3.00 postage = **£57.96**

A trade discount of 30% is also available to bookshops.

Postage rates apply to the UK only. Overseas orders will have any extra postage added and be sent at the airmail 'printed papers' rate, unless you specify otherwise.

❏ I would like to order ... copy(ies) of ***Managing Organisational Change***

and

❏ I enclose my cheque, payable to the Office for Public Management for .... (£24.10 each inc. p&p)

or

❏ I have completed my details for payment by credit card (Visa or Mastercard)

or

❏ Please invoice my organisation at the address below.

Other books in the *Inside Managing for Social Result* series

❏ I would also like . . . copy(ies) of ***Managing Strategy*** (£24.10 each inc. p&p)

❏ I would also like . . . copy(ies) of ***Managing People and Performance*** (£24.10 each inc. p&p)

❏ As I have ordered all three books in the series, I have deducted 20% (before postage) (£57.96 inc. p&p)

Name: ....

Address: ....

[If you are paying by credit card, this must be the ***full billing address*** for your card]

....

.... Postcode: ....

Tel: (& ext.) .... Reference (if any) ....

(in case we need to contact you about your order)

Payment by Visa or MasterCard Please accept my payment by ❏ Visa ❏ Mastercard

Card Number ____ ____ ____ ____

Name on card .... **Expiry date** ....

Signature ....

Please ensure that the address you have given is your full card billing address.
For your security, we will only post books to that address.

OPM, 252B Gray's Inn Road, London, WC1X 8XG
tel: 020 7239 7800; fax 020 7239 0901;
email: publications@opm.co.uk